Saint Malo & Mont St-Michel
Travel Guide

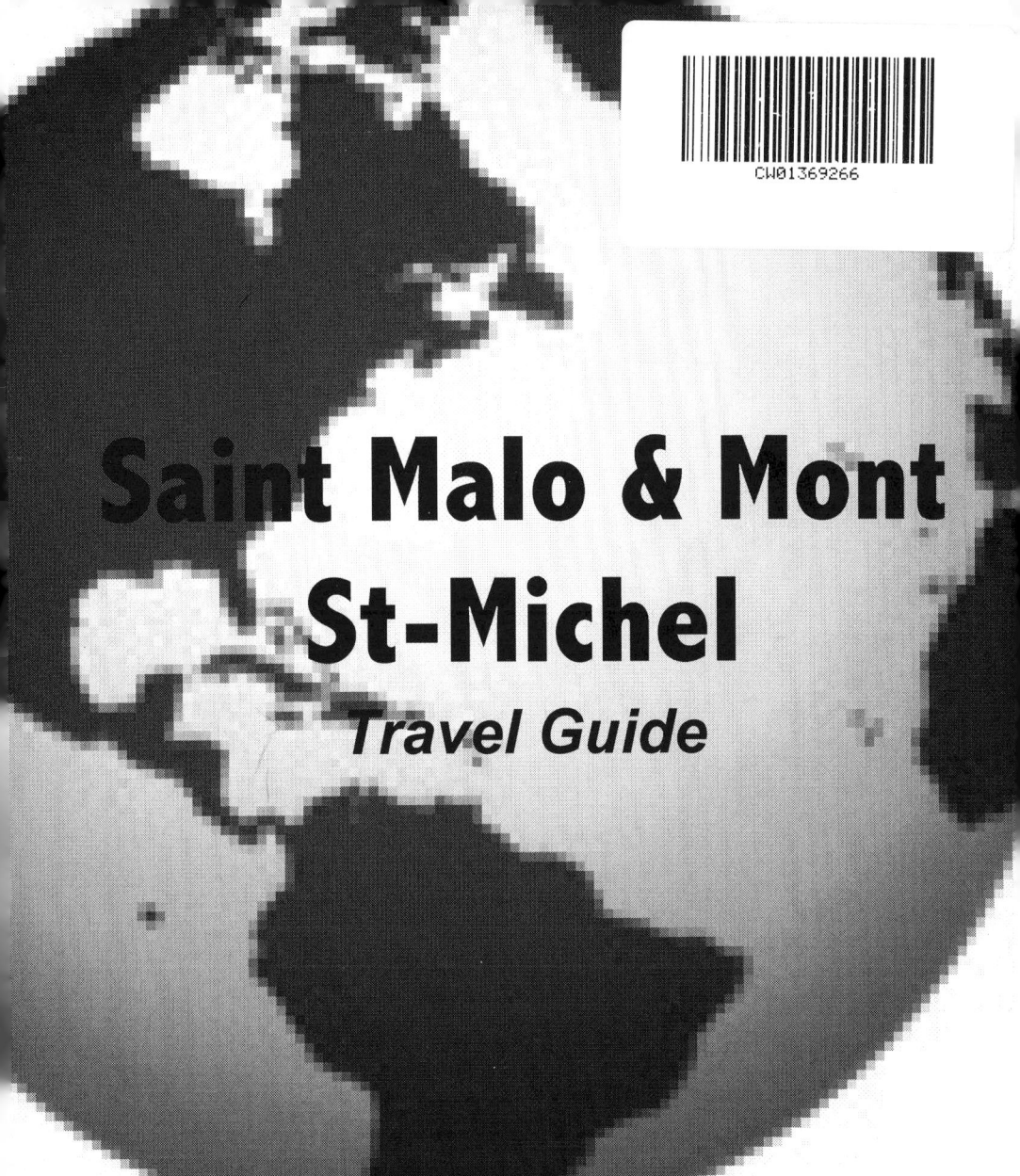

Quick Trips Series

No part of this publication may be reproduced, stored in a retrieval system, or transmitted, in any form or by any means without the prior written permission of the publisher, nor be otherwise circulated in any form of binding or cover other than that in which it is published and without similar condition being imposed on the subsequent purchaser. If there are any errors or omissions in copyright acknowledgements the publisher will be pleased to insert the appropriate acknowledgement in any subsequent printing of this publication. Although we have taken all reasonable care in researching this book we make no warranty about the accuracy or completeness of its content and disclaim all liability arising from its use.

Copyright © 2016, Astute Press
All Rights Reserved.

Table of Contents

ST. MALO & MONT ST-MICHEL — 6
- 🌐 CUSTOMS & CULTURE 9
- 🌐 GEOGRAPHY 12
- 🌐 WEATHER & BEST TIME TO VISIT 13

SIGHTS & ACTIVITIES: WHAT TO SEE & DO — 15
- 🌐 SAINT MALO 15
  - Grand Aquarium 18
  - Mémorial 39–45 19
  - St Vincent Cathedral 20
  - Jacques Cartier 21
  - Jacques Cartier Manor House 22
  - Statue of Robert Surcouf 23
  - Tour Solidor & Musée du Long cours Cap Horniers 24
  - Etoile du Roy 26
  - House of Poets & Writers 26
  - Malouinière de la Chipaudière 27
  - Beaches of St Malo 28
  - Fort National, Grand Bé & Petit Bé 30
  - Les Rochers Sculptes 32
- 🌐 CANCALE 33
- 🌐 MONT SAINT MICHEL 34

Abbey	37
Cloisters	38
Maritime Museum	39
Alligator Bay Reptilarium	40
Sculpture Bay	41

🌐 DINARD 42

🌐 THE RANCE ESTUARY 44

Le Moulin du Prat 44

🌐 DINAN 45

BUDGET TIPS · 48

🌐 ACCOMMODATION 48

Hotel Quic-en-Groigne 48
Hotel du Palais 49
Outside the Walls 50
Brit Hotel Le Surcouf 50
B&B Saint Malo 50
Camping near St Malo 51

🌐 RESTAURANTS, CAFÉS & BARS 53

Salon de the Bergamote Saint Malo Restaurant 53
Other Eateries in Saint Malo 54
Dining in Mont St Michel 55

🌐 SHOPPING 56

Shopping in Saint Malo 56
Shops at Mont St Michel 57
Espices Olivier Roelinger 58

KNOW BEFORE YOU GO · 60

🌐 ENTRY REQUIREMENTS 60

🌐 HEALTH INSURANCE 61

🌐 TRAVELLING WITH PETS 61

🌐 AIRPORTS 62

- AIRLINES 64
- CURRENCY 65
- BANKING & ATMS 65
- CREDIT CARDS 66
- TOURIST TAXES 66
- RECLAIMING VAT 67
- TIPPING POLICY 67
- MOBILE PHONES 68
- DIALLING CODE 69
- EMERGENCY NUMBERS 69
- TIME ZONE 70
- DAYLIGHT SAVINGS TIME 70
- SCHOOL HOLIDAYS 70
- DRIVING LAWS 71
- DRINKING LAWS 72
- SMOKING LAWS 72
- ELECTRICITY 72
- FOOD & DRINK 73

SAINT MALO & MONT ST-MICHEL TRAVEL GUIDE

St. Malo & Mont St-Michel

Here be pirates. Seafaring maps of old might well have included this warning note regarding the port of Saint Malo, as the most memorable chapter of this fortified city was written during the 17th and 18th century, when its cobbled streets witnessed the regular passing of corsairs and pirates, dragging the fabulous booty of treasures from East and West in their wake.

Today, remnants of the era can still be glimpsed in forts, museums and popular culture that tell of the maritime exploits of Jean-François Roberval, René Duguay-Trouin and Robert Surcouf, but also of Jacques Cartier's groundbreaking voyages to the New World.

SAINT MALO & MONT ST-MICHEL TRAVEL GUIDE

Today, despite the historical features, Saint Malo remains a working port, facilitating a fair portion of ferry travel between Britain and France. It is equipped to process various types of cargo, participates in the region's fishing trade and has an extended marina area with 2,000 berths.

Particularly favourable, is its close proximity to the Channel Islands, which can easily be reached for a day trip or short stay. Saint Malo is also conveniently close to

SAINT MALO & MONT ST-MICHEL TRAVEL GUIDE

Mont St Michel, one of France's most popular tourist attractions and visitors with a little more time on their hands, would be well advised to explore other settlements along the Rance Estuary such as Dinard, Dinan and Cancale.

For holidaymakers, St Malo offers access to several beaches and a variety of water-based activities. These include sailing, kayaking and sand surfing. There is a surf and sailing school at Thermes Marins, which can equip you for a number of water and beach sports. If you prefer your sports on land, visit the St Malo Hotel Golf and Country Club (http://www.golf-brittany.com/). Its facilities include a first class 27-hole golf course near Mesnil forest. The land once belonged to one of the most famous of St Malo's privateers, Robert Surcouf, and players can still glimpse his distinctive flag of old.

SAINT MALO & MONT ST-MICHEL TRAVEL GUIDE

Anyone with even a passing interest in history, will find the city's multi-layered role in Western European power struggles intriguing and those with an interest in maritime history or the military architecture of the Middle Ages, will be drawn to the historical heart of Intramuras, the older part of the city found within the walls. Another enigma lies in the unique tidal system. Due to its location, the region experiences some of the highest differences between high and low tide.

🌍 Customs & Culture

The area of Brittany has been settled by various groupings of Celts, from pre-Roman times, and again, at the time of the Anglo-Saxon invasion of England during the 5th to 6th century. Saint Malo allegedly got its name from a Welsh monk, named Maclou or Malo, who fled to

SAINT MALO & MONT ST-MICHEL TRAVEL GUIDE

the region during the 6th century and later became the bishop of Aleth. Although the official language is French, the region still has a number of Breton speakers. The Breton language is similar to Gaelic and the region's folklore celebrates cultural roots with figures from Celtic myth such as Merlin and King Arthur. Another prominent archetype is that of the corsair or privateer.

The New World, or the Americas exerts a subtle influence on the city of Saint Malo. Its maritime heroes, most notably Jacques Cartier, played a vital role in the discovery and colonization of Canada. Additionally, the literary works of François-René de Chateaubriand clearly show his fascination with America, which is echoed in his writings.

SAINT MALO & MONT ST-MICHEL TRAVEL GUIDE

Today, a number of institutions and events still celebrate ties between Canada and Saint Malo. An example of this is Transat Québec-Saint Malo is a trans-Atlantic yacht race that takes place every four years from Quebec City to Saint Malo. The first race in 1984 marked the 450th anniversary of Jacques Cartier's famous voyage. Maison de Quebec, another monument to the connection between Saint Malo and Canada, features a photographic exhibition of various parts of Quebec. It is also available for related events such as lectures and film screenings.

Saint Malo has a lively calendar of events and festivals, centered around various themes and interests including pop rock, jazz, classical music, literature, food, history, nautical activities and Breton culture in general. A favorite game is petanque, a game played with steel balls.

SAINT MALO & MONT ST-MICHEL TRAVEL GUIDE

Seafood is an important mainstay of Breton cuisine, but the region also produces high quality dairy products and indulges a secret sweet tooth in *kouign amann* and *gateau Breton*. Crêpes and galettes, or sweet and savoury pancakes are a regional favorite and you will find plenty of crêperies for affordable eats. Unlike other parts of France, it produces virtually no wine, but brews excellent cider, which is considered the regional beverage of choice.

In fact, a nearby town, Plaudihen Sur Rance is known as the cider capital and has a museum dedicated to apples and cider. Excellent cider is available throughout St Malo and surroundings. You may want to familiarize yourself with a few terms associated with cider. *Cidre de table* refers to a regular table cider, whereas *cidre bouché* indicates a higher quality brew. *Cidre Nouveau* is a new cider and *poiré* is used for a specific type of cider, brewed from pears instead of apples.

🌐 Geography

Saint Malo has a population of around 47,000 and is located in the region of Brittany, on a granite outcrop, in the northwestern part of France. It occupies the right bank of the Rance estuary, along the French side of the English Channel.

A direct ferry service connects Saint Malo with Portsmouth, with three crossings per day. A regular ferry service (http://www.directferries.co.uk/st_malo_ferry.htm) also covers Jersey, Guernsey, Plymouth and Weymouth. Ryanair (http://www.ryanair.com/en/flights-to-dinard/) operates regular flights to Dinard, which is about 12km

SAINT MALO & MONT ST-MICHEL TRAVEL GUIDE

from Saint Malo. A taxi service from the airport at Dinard costs about €20.

Saint Malo is also linked to an intercity bus service (http://www.tibus.fr/) that travels throughout Brittany. A single ticket costs €2. A fun way to explore the inner city of Saint Malo, is via the Vagabond Train, which offers visitors a 30 minute historical tour that would include information on some of the city's maritime history, the French East India Company and the time of the Corsairs.

Dinard can be reached from Saint Malo via the D168, which crosses the bay through a low pontoon bridge. There is a shuttle tour service from Bayeux to Mont St Michel (http://www.bayeuxshuttle.com/mont-saint-michel.htm), which includes commentary on various landmarks and free Wi-Fi on the shuttle, for €60. Day trips

SAINT MALO & MONT ST-MICHEL TRAVEL GUIDE

to the monastery can also be organized from Paris. It is about a 4 hour drive from Paris. It can be reached from Normandy, Brittany and Rennes, via the A84 Caen-Rennes motorway. Although only 57km from Saint Malo, Mont St Michel lies in the neighboring region of Normandy.

🌍 Weather & Best Time to Visit

Saint Malo enjoys a maritime climate that is characterized by warm summers and mild winters. Its weather is moderated by the presence of the British Channel and the warm Gulf Steam that flows through it. July and August are generally the warmest months, with day temperatures in the mid 20s and night temperatures between 13 and 14 degrees Celsius are average, although highs of up to 33 degrees Celsius have been recorded.

SAINT MALO & MONT ST-MICHEL TRAVEL GUIDE

Average day temperatures in spring range from 11 degrees Celsius in March, to 13 degrees Celsius in April and 16 degrees Celsius in May. Winters are cool and cloudy, with average temperatures between 8 and 3 degrees Celsius. This period also sees a lot of rainfall. You can expect day averages of 20 degrees Celsius in September, 16 degrees Celsius in October and a cool 11 degrees Celsius in November.

When visiting some of the attractions in Saint Malo, do bear in mind that outside the holiday sessions, many of the city's museums and other sights hold limited hours and often, guided tours can only be scheduled during the early to mid afternoon. Since the weather tends to be gloomy in winter, many hotels and restaurants close over this period. Do double-check opening times, when scheduling a visit or tour.

SAINT MALO & MONT ST-MICHEL TRAVEL GUIDE

Sights & Activities: What to See & Do

🌐 Saint Malo

Situated on a fortified island, the city of Saint Malo is a major attraction in Brittany. In early times, Saint Malo was linked to the mainland only by way of a slender causeway of sand. Its strategic shoreline location may have something to do with its residents' fierce independence; it

SAINT MALO & MONT ST-MICHEL TRAVEL GUIDE

certainly has everything to do with the city's maritime history and dominance of the seas.

Saint Malo was widely known as the capital of corsairs. What is a Corsair? It is a private ship owner who raids enemy ships, for commercial gain, usually with the official sanction of his country. This is actually where the name comes from. A corsair's "Lettre de course" was literally his licence to piracy. The city's sailors were among the earliest Europeans to reach the New World.

Saint Malo officially became a base for Corsairs (as well as true pirates) from 1144, when the bishop Jean de Châtillon allocated right of asylum to those who sought sanctuary in the city. For several centuries, the free port of Saint Malo prospered as a capital of the Corsairs, under an unofficial motto that went 'Neither Breton, nor

SAINT MALO & MONT ST-MICHEL TRAVEL GUIDE

French, but from Saint Malo I am'. The 'course' came to an end during the early to mid 1800s.

There is plenty to see and do in Saint Malo. One great way of exploring the city is by taking a stroll along the ramparts. There are eight gates, of which the main and most important one is the Grand Porte. The circular route is about 2km long. You can start in the Chateau de St-Malo, a 14th century castle that today houses a museum of the city's history, including artefacts from the age of the corsairs, various aspects of maritime trade and warfare, the deep-sea cod fishing industry off Newfoundland and a special focus on some of St Malo's more colorful adventurers such as Surcouf and Duguay-Trouin. Be sure to check out the view from its watchtowers.

SAINT MALO & MONT ST-MICHEL TRAVEL GUIDE

If you're looking for more maritime history, the Solidor Tower to the west of the city houses a nautical collection. If you want to see the oldest sections of the city, visit Porte St Thomas Gate and go up to Rue du Pelicot, where some wooden buildings that survived a huge fire in 1661 can be found.

The place Vauban has a tropical aquarium, built into its ramparts which you might want to check out, but do not confuse it with the Grand Aquarium on the edge of town. Admission is €6. This is also known as Aquarium Intra Muras.

Grand Aquarium

Rue de Général Patton

Tel: 02 99 21 19 00

http://www.aquarium-st-malo.com/

SAINT MALO & MONT ST-MICHEL TRAVEL GUIDE

This aquarium – the second most visited tourist site in Brittany – brings some of the sea life to shore in a gigantic circular exhibition space that provides visitors with a 360 degree view of fascinating creatures such as Australian bull sharks, zebra sharks, loggerhead turtles and eagle rays. Another display offers a rare glimpse at a collection of shark eggs and embryos. There is a touch pool, where kids can interact with crabs, starfish and mussels.

Among its 11,000 marine animals you will see an impressive shark tank, a school of deadly piranhas, cowfish, lionfish, eels, jellyfish and sea horses. Another highlight is taking an underwater trip aboard the Nautibus, a bright submarine that lets you explore marine life within their own environment. There is a gift shop and the staff speak English. Admission is €16. The Grand Aquarium is located about 4km south of the city center.

Mémorial 39–45

35400 Saint Malo, France

Tel: +33 (0) 2 99 82 41 74

http://www.ville-Saint Malo.fr/culture/les-musees/memorial-3945/#googtrans/fr/en

Fort de la Cité was built during the 18th century, but because of the strategic location of the port at Saint Malo, it became a German military base during World War Two. Today, the bunker in the courtyard houses the Memorial 39/45. The displays are spread across three levels with ten rooms and includes photographs of the period, weaponry, authentic models and other documentation. The tour includes a 45 minute documentary film. Outside the high season months of July and August, the hours are limited. Admission is €6. The cliff top location with its breath-taking seascapes is popular with local residents.

St Vincent Cathedral

Place J de Chantillon, 35400 Saint Malo, France

St Vincent of Saragosse Cathedral, originally a Benedictine Abbey, was built in Romanesque style during the 12th century and elements of this can still be seen in the arches and ribbed vaults that characterize the nave and the transept. From the 13th century, Gothic features were added, and these represent different periods of the Gothic movement. There are various beautiful examples of stained glass art, including its rose window, a fairly recent addition, which was designed by Raymond Cornon.

SAINT MALO & MONT ST-MICHEL TRAVEL GUIDE

A Virgin and Child in white marble dates back to the 18th century. During the Revolution, some features such as the episcopal seat, was removed. The central tower with its Gothic spire was restored from funds given by Napoleon III. There is a memorial for the Saint Malo explorer Jacques Cartier, as well as his tomb and that of naval Lieutenant General René Duguay-Trouin. The church suffered considerable damage during World War Two, and has seen extensive restoration work in recent years.

There are remnants of other religious structures in Saint Malo. At 5 Rue Saint Benoist, a plaque marks the ruins of the Church of the Monastery of St Benedict, constructed between 1626 and 1705. Near Hotel Dieu, the chapel of Saint-Sauveur, another 18th century church, is now used for music concerts and special exhibitions.

Jacques Cartier

Saint Malo was the birthplace of Jacques Cartier, a famous French navigator who explored sections of Canada during his three voyages to the New World. On his first voyage, he landed at Newfoundland and discovered Prince Edward Island. He reached the areas now known as Quebec and Montreal during subsequent voyages by travelling along the St Lawrence river. A third voyage was to have established a colony, but this proved ill-fated, largely due to Cartier's abandonment of the would-be settlers. He is credited as one of the first explorers to realize that the Americas were separate continents, and not a part of Asia.

Today, Saint Malo remembers this former son of the city in a number of ways. There is a monument financed by the Canadian government and the history museum of Saint Malo has a portrait painting of the explorer, as well as a model of his ships. Those interested in his legacy may wish to visit the museum of his former home or paying homage at the statue of Cartier, which stands at Bastion de la Holland and gazes out towards the Rance estuary.

Jacques Cartier Manor House

Manoir de Limoëlou,

Rue David MacDonald Stewart, 35400 Saint Malo, France

Tel: 02 99 40 97 73

The explorer's former residence has been restored to a house museum that accurately reflects a typical household of the 16th century. Visitors will be able to view Cartier's bedroom, the kitchen, as well as a display of navigational instruments in the map room. There is a bust of Cartier. The facility is only open to the public for two daily guided tours at 10am and 3pm. Admission is €6. While the tour is in French, English material is available. Arrangements can be made by emailing Musee.Jacques.Cartier@wanadoo.fr

Statue of Robert Surcouf

https://foursquare.com/v/statue-robert-surcouf/4fca4e8be4b04ba0d0f7951c

A statue in Saint Malo commemorates Robert Surcouf, the last and perhaps most famous of the Corsairs. Surcouf was born into "corsair nobility", with notorious corsairs such as René Duguay-Trouin and Robert Surcouf de Maisonneuve represented on both sides of his lineage.

He grew up to partake in several swashbuckling exploits in the Indian Ocean, most notably the capture of the *Triton* and the *Kent*, before returning to Saint Malo. When he died, he left his heirs an estate worth around 2 million francs. The sculpture of Robert Surcouf in Saint Malo is the work of Alfred Caravanniez. It faces the English Channel and was inaugurated in 1903.

Tour Solidor & Musée du Long cours Cap Horniers

Quai Solidor, 35400 Saint Malo, France

Tel: 02 99 40 71 58

Tour Solidor was originally constructed by Duke Jean IV of Brittany, between 1369 and 1382, as means of controlling access to Saint Malo. The whole complex consists of three towers, linked via curtain walls to a central fortified dungeon. The existing bastion includes sections of salvaged Gallo-Roman masonry. The steps are quite steep, but the tower offers magnificent views of the surrounding landscape.

Tour Solidor is located in the town of Saint-Servan, which was once an independent city, but has now fully merged with Saint Malo. In its time, it served as fort and prison, but today it houses a museum dedicated to the brave explorers who had opened up the route around Cape Horn.

The passage around Cape Horn is one of the most hazardous ship routes in the world. Fierce wind, rogue waves and the presence of ice all contribute to its perils. Through a wide range of informative displays, the museum sheds some light onto the difficulties and challenges of these long voyages. Exhibits include ship models, ship's instruments, log books, items made by the sailors and souvenirs from the New World. The museum provides insight into sailing conditions and discusses the importance of some of the cargo carried. Admission is €6.

Etoile du Roy

Quai Duguay Trouin 35400 Saint Malo

Tel: 02 99 40 48 72

http://www.etoile-du-roy.com/

Catch a real glimpse into the life of a corsair and get your sea legs aboard the Etoile du Roy or Royal Star, a replica of a real 18th century corsair's vessel. The frigate is 47m long, has 20 cannons of firepower, three masts and can accommodate a crew of 240. The ship is open for tours and can also be hired for a variety of events. Admission for a dockside tour is €6.

House of Poets & Writers

5 Rue du Pélicot, St Malo

Tel: 00 33 2 99 40 28 77

http://www.Saint Malo-tourisme.co.uk/stay/what-to-do/art-culture/137774-maison-internationale-des-poetes-et-des-ecrivains

The building dates back to 1676, and while many of the city's structures have been rebuilt with stone, it is one of the few wood-fronted houses remaining. From 1990, the building has been used to showcase various literary initiatives, such as exhibitions, workshops, conferences and literary themed walks. Administered under UNESCO, it is open from 2 to 6pm, Tuesdays to Saturdays throughout the year.

Malouinière de la Chipaudière

La Chipaudière, 35400, Saint Malo

Tel: +332 99 81 61 41

Malouinière de la Chipaudière was built by François-Auguste Magon de la Lande, one of the most powerful ship owners of the area and a director of the French East India Company. The mansion was constructed between 1710 and 1720 and includes oak wood panelling from Holland and Norway.

The garden is spread across several levels and terraces and includes ponds, moats, paths lined with lime trees and even a chapel. The property was classified a historical monument in 1982. It is still owned by the Magon family. Although not generally open to the public,

SAINT MALO & MONT ST-MICHEL TRAVEL GUIDE

guided tours can be arranged during the holiday season by emailing magon-de-la-giclais.nicolas@orange.fr. Admission is €5.

Beaches of St Malo

Plage du Mole is located at the foot of the city's ramparts between Bastion de la Hollande and Mole des Noires jetty, a jetty of 500m which shelters it from the winds. Popular for swimming, it can get quite crowded during summer.

Plage de Bon Secours is larger and can be reached through the Porte St-Piere gate at the northern side of the Bastion de la Hollande. The beach has a protected seawater pool, Piscine de Bon with a diving platform and visitors can rent kayaks and catamarans from a beach

SAINT MALO & MONT ST-MICHEL TRAVEL GUIDE

club on the ramparts. There is also a beach bar for snacks and refreshments.

Grand Plage, the main sandy beach extends over 3km, towards the coastal town of Parame. It is lined with hotels to cater to the needs of tourists wishing to stay near Saint Malo, but outside the city walls. Visitors wishing to stroll towards Rochebonne Paramé, will be treated to a brilliant overview of Saint Malo and surroundings. Opposite Fort Nationale, it connects with another beach, Plage de l'Eventail, which is somewhat rockier.

According to tradition, Plage de l'Eventail was a favorite haunt of François-René de Chateaubriand, a famous French writer who was born in Saint Malo. During low tide, you can walk from Plage de l'Eventail to Fort National, a popular activity for tourists.

Fort National, Grand Bé & Petit Bé

With its granite walls and square structure, Fort National was added to the defensive structures of Saint Malo towards the end of the seventeenth century by the military architect Sebastien Le Prestre de Vauban. Originally the site was used as a lighthouse, a gallows and allegedly a battery. Vauban's fort was constructed by Siméon Garangeau.

It withstood early attacks in 1693 and 1695, and was modified, adding a lower battery without embrasures, that was better able to fire on moving targets. Fort National was the largest of a circle of fortification that included similar structures on Grand Bé and Petit Bé. Among its facilities was a barracks to house soldiers and a cistern

SAINT MALO & MONT ST-MICHEL TRAVEL GUIDE

for collecting rainwater. Fort National was also known as the Royal Fort.

During low tide, walk out to the Bé islands (carefully). On Petit Bé you'll find a well-placed fort built in the 17th century to keep the British and Dutch away. When visiting Petit Bé, be sure to check out the models of other forts in the bay, as well as designs which clearly show the evolution of Petit Bé's fortification.

On Grand Bé you'll find the tomb of Chateaubriand, the poet, diplomat, father of French Romanticism in literature and gourmet who gave his name to a delicious cut of steak. François-René de Chateaubriand is a well respected literary representative of the French Romantic movement, but his career included a number of other interesting chapters. During a visit to the United States, he interviewed George Washington and lived for a time with a group of Native Americans.

For a time, he served in various diplomatic posts under Napoleon Bonaparte and also attracted the favour of Russian Tsarina Elizabeth Alexeievna. He even served as ambassador to Prussia and England, but withdrew from public life towards the end of his life, requesting that he be buried on the island of Grand Bé. His grave is marked by a simple cross, overlooking the sea and can only be reached at low tide.

From the top of the Grand Bé you'll also enjoy beautiful views of the entire Emerald Coast. Some of the other islands in the vicinity include Rimains, which housed another bastion of Vauban, Cézembre, which was one of the most heavily bombarded areas during World War Two and De Guesclin island, located between Saint Malo and Cancale, associated with the well-known Breton de Guesclin family and also the English king John Lockland.

Les Rochers Sculptes

Sentier du Littoral, Saint Malo, France

An enigmatic feature near Saint Malo is Les Rochers Sculptes. The impressive collection of rock sculptures were created during the 1800s by Abbé Adolphe-Julien Fouré, a hermit monk of the region, who had lost his hearing and speech. There are over 300 pieces carved into the granite rocks at Rotheneuf, portraying pirates, smugglers, adventurers, fishermen and assorted monsters.

SAINT MALO & MONT ST-MICHEL TRAVEL GUIDE

Some of the imagery is focussed on the notorious Rotheneuf family, a smugglers clan active in the region from the 15th to 18th century. It is said that the monk was also a talented woodcarver, but little of his work in this medium survived. The area can be visited for €2.50. Besides the artwork, you can enjoy great views of the ocean here. Les Rocher Sculptes is located approximately 5km from Thermes Marins, towards Cancale.

🌎 Cancale

While in St.-Malo, why not take the opportunity to explore the nearby town of Cancale. This beautiful fishing village is widely known as "the oyster capital" of Brittany. The same Cancale oysters that Louis XIV had sent to Versailles on horseback, can now be enjoyed in any number of restaurants while gazing out across the bay towards Mont St. Michel in the distance.

Two well known artists immortalized Cancale in their works. Eugène Feyen received praise for his highly developed sense of perception from none other than Vincent van Gogh. The other artist is the American John Singer Sargent. One great way of enjoying the picturesque surroundings is by taking the circular route from the town to Point du Grouin. You will see the bird sanctuary at Île des Landes, as well as Mont St Michel in the distance.

Mont Saint Michel

The unique tidal island and town of Mont Saint Michel is one of the most popular tourist attractions in France, second only to the Eiffel Tower. It is located, just off of the

SAINT MALO & MONT ST-MICHEL TRAVEL GUIDE

coast of Normandy at the mouth of the Couesnon River. The tide which flows between the English Channel and the Couesnon River can change rapidly and vary by as much 14 meters (46 feet) between high tide and low tide. Victor Hugo compared the swiftness of the tide to that of a "galloping horse". There have been instances of people who have drowned by straying too far after ignoring the warning signs and tidal schedules. The tidal mudflats are also known to hide areas of quicksand that can be dangerous.

The distance from the coast of Normandy to the island is only about one-half mile and free shuttle buses make the trip every few minutes. The famous island is just 247 acres in size, and its landscape is dominated by the Mont Saint Michel Abbey. The town of Mont Saint Michel sits just below one of France's most recognizable landmarks, the Abbey of Mont Saint Michel.

One writer noted when viewing Mont Saint Michel from the mainland that it "seems to float on the sea as gracefully as a ship under full sail, catching all the changing colors of the clouds." The highest point of the mountainous island is 92 meters (301 feet). Mont St Michel has been declared a UNESCO World Heritage Site.

The monastery's connection to Normandy and Norman politics goes back to the 900s, but in 1065, it prominently lent its support to William the Conqueror's campaign to ascend to the English throne. It is also depicted in the famous Bayeux tapestry. Several centuries later, however, the English failed to take the monastery, thanks

SAINT MALO & MONT ST-MICHEL TRAVEL GUIDE

to modified fortification. Les Michelettes, two bombards that remain from their failed efforts, can still be viewed by the public.

Grand Rue is the narrow and sloping main street of Mont St Michel and this is accessibly via Porte de l'Avancee, the main gate from the causeway. From the 12th century, it was the route followed by pilgrims, but today, it is crowded with tourists and lined with restaurants, inns and souvenir shops. Many of its buildings date back to the 15th or 16th century.

Over three million people visit each year and for those that want to spend a night on the island, there are hotels, but they are much more expensive than those in the surrounding towns. There is a scenic route up the ramparts, via stairs, which provides great views and photo opportunities to capture the surrounding scenery. A third route, via Porte Eschaugette to the left of the main gate, will take you away from the maddening crowd.

Abbey

The Abbey sits at the top of Mont Saint Michel. According to legend, this was once the setting of a fierce battle between the devil and the Archangel Michael, and early pilgrims had to brave treacherous quicksand and listen to the tolling of a guiding bell to reach the holy site. It is a stunning monument and offers tremendous views of Normandy, as well as Brittany, which is just a few kilometers away.

The Abbey and the town is so beautiful that its image has been recreated on millions of postcards.

The oldest section of the abbey can be found to the northwest of the rock settlement. Romanesque in character, this was completed in the 11th century and includes Les chapels Saint Martin and Notre Dame Thirty Candles, the oldest sections of the abbey. What was once the monks' dormitory, now serves as a bookshop.

Cloisters

Mont Saint Michel cloister is located next to the Abbey. It was the last part of the complex to be completed in 1228. While secluded from the outside world, the cloister serves as the center and heart of monastic existence. It is connected to key areas such as refectory, kitchen, church, dormitory and stairways.

The cloister is a place of solitude and peacefulness that has an aura of spirituality. The cloister is surrounded by

SAINT MALO & MONT ST-MICHEL TRAVEL GUIDE

two rows of staggered columns on four sides. The staggered columns were designed to spread the weight of the cloister over a wide area because of the crypts and halls below. While the Abbey was constructed of granite some of the cloister's walls are limestone, and the elegant 13th century columns are made of marble.

In the center of the cloister is a meticulously maintained garden that dates back to the 13th century and holds a variety of herbaceous plants. When you emerge from the hallways into the garden, you will be stunned by the burst of light and bright colors. It will seem as if the walls of the cloister exist for the protection of the garden. The lush green garden seems to open up to the heavens, and it is easy to understand why it would be an ideal place for prayer and meditation.

SAINT MALO & MONT ST-MICHEL TRAVEL GUIDE

The island monastery has a permanent population of between 30 and 40. During the spring and summer seasons, Mont Saint Michel hosts over 20,000 tourists per day, and visiting early in the morning or late in the afternoon is the best way to avoid the crowds. Mont Saint Michel is a unique historical and spiritual monument that is well worth a visit.

Maritime Museum

Mont-St-Michel, France

If you are fascinated by the unique tidal system of the Mont St Michel Bay and the maritime history of the area, you may wish to pay a visit to the maritime museum. There is a graphic presentation explaining the complex seaside eco-system as well, as a short documentary video on hydraulics and related engineering. Exhibits include various miniature ship models. Admission is €9. Do bear in mind that commentary is available only in French.

Alligator Bay Reptilarium

Road to Pontorson, Mont Saint Michel, France

Tel: +33 02 3368 1118

http://www.alligator-bay.com/?page_id=488

Alligator Bay is the name of a Reptilarium located just off Mont St Michel. It has one of the most exceptional collections of reptiles in Europe. A selection of around 300 tortoises and turtles, including several giant species from Africa, reside in a raised park. The alligator enclosures can be navigated via a series of walkways and bridges. There are approximately 200 different species of alligators and crocodiles, including albinos, as well as giant pythons and other snakes and lizards. There are also dedicated picnic areas. Admission is €12.50.

Sculpture Bay

La Bruyère, Mont St Michel

Tel: 02 99 48 12 77

http://www.sculpturesdelabaie.com

Conceived about 15 years ago, Sculpture Bay seeks to exhibit and inform about the art of sculpture through the creation of an innovative and ever changing sculpture garden. Many of the works represented are of local Caen stone, but there are also bronze pieces and wood-carvings. Contributing artists include Bertram Wawera and Martine Latimier. Sculpture Bay is open to the public from Easter till the end of September.

🌐 Dinard

Continuing down the Emerald Coast, on the opposite bank of the Rance River, lies Dinard. During the 19th century, this humble fishing village was transformed into a glittering seaside playground for British aristocrats and wealthy Americans. Lingering Victorian charm has ensured that it remains one of the most "British" seaside resorts in France. (In fact, the town holds a Festival of British Cinema during the first week of October).

In keeping with its genteel pedigree, this is a beach town known for its sophistication, rather than a loud party atmosphere. Dinard has many excellent restaurants and bars, and if you fancy testing the favor of Lady Luck, you'll definitely want to check out the Casino Barriere de Dinard (http://www.lucienbarriere.com/fr/Casino/Dinard/accueil.html), the largest casino in Brittany. Enjoy dinner at the

SAINT MALO & MONT ST-MICHEL TRAVEL GUIDE

restaurant, a typical French brasserie overlooking the town's biggest beach (Plage de l'Écluse), then try your luck at one of the slot machines.

Also at Plage de l'Écluse, you will find the Wishbone Club (http://www.wishbone-club-dinard.com/), which offers facilities for sailing, windsurfing and kayaking. Lessons and equipment rentals can be arranged. For great sea views, take a stroll along the Promenade de Clair du Lune, which hugs the shoreline passing Pointe du Moulinet, Plage du Prieuré, Plage de l'Écluse and Plage de St-Énogat. There are plenty of benches to sit down and enjoy the stunning scenery or the backdrop of cliff-top mansions dating back to the 19th century.

The Dinard Golf Club (http://www.dinardgolf.com/site/main.html) is located in the nearby town of Saint-Briac-sur-Mer. It is one of the oldest courses on continental Europe and is beautifully situated along the sea.

The Dinard Street Market trades at the Central Square and offers the opportunity to sample a number of local specialities, such as oysters, sheep's milk cheese, bread, fish, fruit, vegetables, olives and more. Besides food, you can also browse through stalls selling clothing, jewellery and leather items.

The Rance Estuary

Le Moulin du Prat

22690 La Vicomté-sur-Rance

Tel: 02 96 83 21 41

http://lavicomtesurrance.free.fr/

SAINT MALO & MONT ST-MICHEL TRAVEL GUIDE

Tidal mills in Europe date back to Roman times and were quite common during the Middle Ages, especially along the Atlantic shorelines. Typically placed in a river estuary, but close enough to the shore to be influenced by tidal action, they were used to power water wheels. Today, a tidal mill can be used to generate electricity.

Le Moulin du Prat is located between Dinan and Saint Malo in the tiny village of La Vicomte sur Rance and it features one of the last tidal mills of Brittany. From the 1800s to the First World War, the mill was used for flour, but after the war, it fell into disrepair. In recent years, though, the local municipality acquired the building and began to restore the mill to working condition. It was inaugurated in 2002 and can be visited by the public between April and mid November. Admission is €3.

Nearby, the Rance tidal power station was opened in 1966, as the world's first facility of its kind. The idea of a tidal power station to utilize the high tides of the Rance area was conceived as early as 1921, but was only realized in the 1960s, through the efforts of Albert Coquot. The power station is open to the public.

🌐 Dinan

Located about 20km to the south of Saint Malo, Dinan is a walled medieval town occupying a hillside overlooking the River Rance. The town has plenty of interesting historical buildings and oozes character. You may need good walking shoes to manage its steep cobbled streets, but a more relaxing way of exploring the town is by boarding Le Petit Train de Dinan (http://www.petit-train-dinan.com/index.php), a tourist train that passes various of

SAINT MALO & MONT ST-MICHEL TRAVEL GUIDE

the town's main attractions, including the basilica, the viaduct and the Place Duclos. Tickets are priced at €6.

The Jardin Anglaise, or English Garden can be found at the upper parts of the walls, by the medieval cemetery. The scenery includes stunning river views and the garden also has a bust of the explorer Auguste Pavie, who was born in Dinan. The castle or chateau of Dinan is also known as the Tower of St Anne's and dates back to the late 14th century. It had served as residence and prison, but today, its museum displays an interesting collection of holy artefacts, furniture, silverware and prehistoric tools. You can enjoy stunning views from the top of the 34m tower. Admission is €4.20.

The Basilique St-Sauveur owes its existence to the promise of a Crusader from Dinan, who vowed to build a church if he ever saw his hometown again. The present structure combines elements of Romanesque, Gothic and Renaissance architecture. In true Gothic style, the church spire is topped by a collection of gargoyles. Some of these granite sculptures are around 800 years old.

The beautifully elaborate stained glass windows, however, date back to the 1940s and are the work of Louis Barrel. An important relic associated with the church is the heart of Bertrant Du Guesclin, a French hero of the Hundred Year War.

The zoo at La Bourbansais houses lions, lemurs, giraffes and more. There is a daily falconry show at 2.30pm, as well as display featuring a pack of hunting hounds. There is a play area for children, a picnic area and cafes serving snacks and meals. It is located in Pleugueneuc, about 10 minutes from Dinan.

There is a weekly market on Thursdays at Place du Champ and Place du Guesclin and a highlight of the cultural calendar is the Fête des Remparts, a two day medieval festival that takes place in July every second year at the chateau. Boat cruises to Dinan are available from Dinard and St Malo. For an affordable stopover in Dinan, consider the Hotel de La Tour de L'Horloge, which is located in the pedestrianized heart of the medieval center at 5 Rue de la Chaux.

SAINT MALO & MONT ST-MICHEL TRAVEL GUIDE

Budget Tips

🌐 Accommodation

Hotel Quic-en-Groigne

8 Rue de Estrees, Saint Malo

Tel: +33 (0)2 99 20 22 20

http://www.quic-en-groigne.com

Located off the cobblestoned streets of Intramuras, Hotel

Quic-en-Groigne is a former family home that has been converted to a small hotel.

It is near various restaurants and shops, as well as several of the city's tourist attractions. Rooms are cosy and comfortable and include bathroom amenities and free internet. Accommodation begins at €83 and includes a continental buffet breakfast.

Hotel du Palais

8 rue Toullier, 35400 Saint Malo, France

Tel: +33 2 99 40 07 30

Hotel du Palais is located at the heart of the historical center, right next to St Vincent Cathedral, and only 200m from the beach. The hotel has a bar/lounge. Rooms include a flat-screen TV, private bathroom and free Wi-Fi.

Accommodation begins at €83. Breakfast is an optional €8.50 extra.

Outside the Walls

Brit Hotel Le Surcouf

17 avenue du Reverend Pere Umbricht,

35400 Saint Malo, France

http://www.surcoufhotel.com/

Brit Hotel Le Surcouf is about 150m from the beach, but 2km from the historical center of the city. The staff are attentive and friendly and the hotel has wheelchair friendly facilities.

Rooms include flat screen TV and free high-speed internet. Accommodation begins at €70. Breakfast is an optional €8 extra.

SAINT MALO & MONT ST-MICHEL TRAVEL GUIDE

B&B Saint Malo

Place de la decouverte,

Avenue du Général de Gaulle,

35 400 Saint Malo, France

Tel: +33 892 78 80 95

http://www.hotel-bb.com/en/hotels/Saint Malo-centre-la-decouverte.htm

Part of the B&B hotel group, B&B Saint Malo is located near the aquarium, but about a 15 minute drive from the ferry port and Intramuras. Rooms include a microwave oven, fridge, flat screen TV and free wireless internet. Accommodation begins at €37 per night. The breakfast buffet is an optional €6 extra.

SAINT MALO & MONT ST-MICHEL TRAVEL GUIDE

Camping near St Malo

Visitors who do not mind roughing it a little, might be tempted to organize accommodation at one of the campgrounds near Saint Malo. Camping la Fontaine (http://www.campinglafontaine.com/campingang.html) is located at 49 Rue Fontaine aux Pelerin, on the outskirts of St Malo.

It offers a number of facilities, including electricity, water, gas, showers, laundry facilities and even facilities for people with disabilities. There is also a heated pool and play area for children. Wi-Fi is available, but charged. There are various accommodation options, including chalets, which can be rented from €54.90 per night or €299 per week or mobile homes, which can be rented from €60.90 per night or €335 per week. Bear in mind that the campsite is near the industrial part of St Malo and may not offer the best of views. Basic camping rates begin at €5,70 per person.

If you have your own motor home, or other camping facilities, it is hard to beat the price at Aire Camping-Cars les Ilots, which is €10 per night for a camp site during the season, and €5 in the off-season, but, although the camping ground is located near the beach and the bus service, facilities are somewhat limited. Aire Camping-Cars les Ilots can be found at Rothéneuf, Avenue de la Guimorais (Tel: +33 2 99 56 98 72).

Camping Municipal La Cite d'Alet is located on Allee Gaston Buy and offers stunning views, electricity, washing, shower and toilet facilities. It is near the ferry port as well as the World War Two museum. Basic site rental is €15 per night. For more information on some of the campsites in the area, go to

http://www.campingfrance.com/UK or

http://www.ukcampsite.co.uk/sites/reviews.asp?revid=8869.

🌐 Restaurants, Cafés & Bars

Salon de the Bergamote Saint Malo Restaurant

3 place Jean de Chatillon, 35400 Saint Malo, France

Tel: +33 (2) 99402814

Located right by the St Vincent Cathedral, Salon de the Bergamote combines friendly service with an interesting decor and great atmosphere. There is a good selection of teas, coffees and cider. On the food side, expect salads, pies, cakes, omelettes, pancakes and galettes. Some of the favorites include the smoked salmon salad, a goats cheese and bacon salad, fig pie, vegetarian quiche and crepe with banana rum ice cream and cream. All crepes are made with buckwheat and gluten free.

Other Eateries in Saint Malo

What sets Autour du Beurre Restaurant apart is its exceptional dairy products. The cheese platter is one of the menu highlights, but what truly renders the restaurant unique is a series of 8 specially flavored homemade butters. Autour du Beurre Restaurant is located at rue de l'orme and serves a three course lunch menu for €18.

Even before the food is on the table, you can feast your eyes on the beautiful and creative decor at Le Creperie des Lutins Restaurant. The eaterie is themed around fairy tale creatures such as witches, fairies and goblins - with menu items being named after magical creatures.

Homemade cider is served and the crepes and galettes are available in seafood, vegetarian and cheesy options. Le Creperie des Lutins Restaurant is located at 7 Grand Rue, within the walls in Saint Malo.

Dining in Mont St Michel

Most of the eateries on Mont St Michel are fairly pricey, but if you are looking for an economical place, try La Sirene (Tel: 02 33 60 08 60), which in located along Grand Rue and specializes in crêpes and galettes. Expect to spend between €12 and €20 for your meal.

Another affordable creperie is Creperie La Cloche (http://www.creperie-le-mont-saint-michel.fr/restaurant-mont-saint-michel) in Rue Principale, which combines friendly service with simple, no-frills homemade pancakes or crêpes. Some of the fillings you can expect range from

Norman sausage with cheese to apple with hot brandy. Meals should cost around €15 per person.

Located near the shuttle stop and several souvenir shops, La Rotisserie Restaurant (8 Route du Mont, Mont St Michel http://www.restaurantlarotisserie-montsaintmichel.com/en/home) is large enough to seat well over 400 and offers a somewhat more varied menu.

Dishes include omelette, fish soup, chicken with mushroom sauce, lamb with potato fritters and delicious dessert options such as profiteroles - ice cream puffs with hot dark chocolate sauce and almonds, as well as meringue. There is a three tier price structure which ranges from the express menu for €13.60 to the La Rôtisserie selections for €28. Lunch dishes cost around €12.20.

🌐 Shopping

Shopping in Saint Malo

Aux Délices Malouins is located at 12 rue St-Vincent (tel. 02-99-40-55-22) and sells chocolate, Breton sweets and biscuits, home made marzipan, cider, liqueurs and other regional favorites. Larnicol G. at 6 rue St-Vincent also sells sweets, chocolates, macaroons. Carré Chocolat at 47 Quai Duguay-Trouin has a large selection of chocolates, truffles, pralines and more in a wide range of flavors and combinations.

At 1 Rue Ste Barbe, you will find the gift shop Coté Remparts. For antiques, visit Henri Néré at 17 Dauphin in Saint Malo or browse at La Petite Brocante at 27 rue Gén de Castelnau. Cinq Semaines en Ballon at 11 Grand Rue in Saint Malo sells various art and craft objects and

Librairie Pasal Galodé Editions at 7 rue de Dinan in Saint Malo stocks books.

Le Comptoir des Cotonniers at 6 rue Broussais in Saint Malo, sells a number of typically Breton craft items, including stoneware and lace, as well as books and CDs. Aux Arts Celtiques at 4 rue de Dinan also sells handcrafted items. If you are interested in books, also visit L'Epigraphe at 3 rue Gardelle or Cultura in avenue Flaudaie. Ondine at 28 Rue Levavasseur (Tel: +33 2 99 46 17 73) in Dinard stocks a good selection of tourist interest books, as well as postcards.

Shops at Mont St Michel

One of the most popular souvenirs to bring home from Mont St Michel is a monk ornament, celebrating the settlement's ties with a religious past. Although not always historically accurate, they make charming Christmas tree decorations. At the monastery bookshop, you can buy a wide range of publications, including fun activity books for children and large, glossy coffee table books. Here, too, you will find souvenirs such as fridge magnets, jewellery and household items.

For goods with a medieval flavor, stray into Diagon Alley, where you can browse through plastic gargoyles or replica Gothic armour. Aux 3 Croissants sells a range of products from Normandy and Brittany. There is a good selection of porcelain, but also medieval ornaments such as monks and knights. Like most businesses, the shop is located on Grand Rue, the settlement's main street.

Espices Olivier Roelinger

1 Rue Duduesclin, Cancale

Tel: +33 2 23 15 13 91

http://www.epices-roellinger.com/

Cancale is the oyster capital, but it is also the home of French chef Olivier Roelinger, who is regarded as one of the foremost authorities on contemporary French cooking. He celebrates the links between Saint Malo's maritime history and the trade route to India and anyone with a particular interest in creating culinary masterpieces, would be advised to visit his spice shop.

You can choose from a huge selection of spices from all over the world, including cinnamon from Madagascar or India, saffron from Morocco, vanilla from Reunion, Uganda or the Comoros, peppers from Sri Lanka and

SAINT MALO & MONT ST-MICHEL TRAVEL GUIDE

chillies from Mexico. The shop also stocks oils, condiments, salts and teas, books and DVDs, speciality utensils and you can even book cooking classes, if you have the time.

SAINT MALO & MONT ST-MICHEL TRAVEL GUIDE

Know Before You Go

🌐 Entry Requirements

By virtue of the Schengen agreement, visitors from other countries in the European Union will not need a visa when visiting France. Additionally Swiss visitors are also exempt. Visitors from certain other countries such as Andorra, Canada, the United Kingdom, Ireland, the Bahamas, Australia, the USA, Chile, Costa Rica, Croatia, El Salvador, Guatemala, Honduras, Israel, Malaysia, Mauritius, Monaco, Nicaragua, New Zealand, Panama, Paraguay, Saint Kitts and Nevis, San Marino, the Holy See, Seychelles, Taiwan and Japan do not need visas for a stay of less than 90 days. Visitors to France must be in possession of a valid passport that expires no sooner than three months after the intended stay. UK citizens will not need a visa to enter France. Visitors must provide proof of residence, financial support and the reason for their visit. If you wish to work or study in France, however, you will need a visa.

🌐 Health Insurance

Citizens of other EU countries are covered for emergency health care in France. UK residents, as well as visitors from Switzerland are covered by the European Health Insurance Card (EHIC), which can be applied for free of charge. Visitors from non-Schengen countries will need to show proof of private health insurance that is valid for the duration of their stay in France (that offers at least €37,500 coverage), as part of their visa application. A letter of coverage will need to be submitted to the French Embassy along with your visa application. American travellers will need to check whether their regular medical insurance covers international travel. No special vaccinations are required.

🌐 Travelling with Pets

France participates in the Pet Travel Scheme (PETS) which allows UK residents to travel with their pets without requiring quarantine upon re-entry. Certain conditions will need to be met. The animal will have to be microchipped and up to date on rabies vaccinations. In the case of dogs, France also requires vaccination against distemper. If travelling from another EU member country, you will need an EU pet passport. Regardless of the country, a Declaration of Non-Commercial Transport must be signed stating that you do not intend to sell your pet.

SAINT MALO & MONT ST-MICHEL TRAVEL GUIDE

A popular form of travel with pets between the UK and France is via the Eurotunnel, which has special facilities for owners travelling with pets. This includes dedicated pet exercise areas and complimentary dog waste bags. Transport of a pet via this medium costs €24. The Calais Terminal has a special Pet Reception Building. Pets travelling from the USA will need to be at least 12 weeks old and up to date on rabies vaccinations. Microchipping or some form of identification tattoo will also be required. If travelling from another country, do inquire about the specific entry requirements for your pet into France and also about re-entry requirements in your own country.

🌍 Airports

There are three airports near Paris where most international visitors arrive. The largest of these is **Charles De Gaulle** (CDG) airport, which serves as an important hub for both international and domestic carriers. It is located about 30km outside Paris and is well-connected to the city's rail network. Most trans-Atlantic flights arrive here. **Orly** (ORY) is the second largest and oldest airport serving Paris. It is located 18km south of the city and is connected to several public transport options including a bus service, shuttle service and Metro rail. Most of its arrivals and departures are to other destinations within Europe. **Aéroport de Paris-Beauvais-Tillé** (BVA), which lies in Tillé near Beauvais, about 80km outside

Paris, is primarily used by Ryanair for its flights connecting Paris to Dublin, Shannon Glasgow and other cities.

There are several important regional airports. **Aéroport Nice Côte d'Azur** (NCE) is the 3rd busiest airport in France and serves as a gateway to the popular French Riviera. **Aéroport Lyon Saint-Exupéry** (LYS) lies 20km east of Lyon and serves as the main hub for connections to the French Alps and Provence. It is the 4th busiest airport of France. **Aéroport de Bordeaux** (BOD) served the region of Bordeaux. **Aéroport de Toulouse – Blagnac** (TLS), which lies 7km from Toulouse, provides access to the south-western part of France. **Aéroport de Strasbourg** (SXB), which lies 10km west of Strasbourg, served as a connection to Orly, Paris and Nice. **Aéroport de Marseille Provence** (MRS) is located in the town of Marignane, about 27km from Marseille and provides access to Provence and the French Riviera. **Aéroport Nantes Atlantique** (NTE) lies in Bouguenais, 8km from Nantes carriers and provides a gateway to the regions of Normandy and Brittany in the western part of France. **Aéroport de Lille** (LIL) is located near Lesquin and provides connections to the northern part of France.

🌐 Airlines

Air France is the national flag carrier of France and in 2003, it merged with KLM. The airline has a Flying Blue rewards

SAINT MALO & MONT ST-MICHEL TRAVEL GUIDE

program, which allows members to earn, accumulate and redeem Flying Blue Miles on any flights with Air France, KLM or any other Sky Team airline. This includes Aeroflot, Aerolineas Argentinas, AeroMexico, Air Europa, Alitalia, China Airlines, China Eastern, China Southern, Czech Airlines, Delta, Garuda Indonesia, Kenya Airways, Korean Air, Middle Eastern Airlines, Saudia, Tarom, Vietnam Airlines and Xiamen Airlines.

Air France operates several subsidiaries, including the low-cost Transavia.com France, Cityjet and Hop! It is also in partnership with Air Corsica. Other French airlines are Corsairfly and XL Airways France (formerly Star Airlines).

France's largest intercontinental airport, Charles de Gaulle serves as a hub for Air France, as well as its regional subsidiary, HOP!. It also functions as a European hub for Delta Airlines. Orly Airport, also in Paris, serves as the main hub for Air France's low cost subsidiary, Transavia, with 40 different destinations, including London, Madrid, Copenhagen, Moscow, Casablanca, Algiers, Amsterdam, Istanbul, Venice, Rome, Berlin and Athens. Aéroport de Marseille Provence (MRS) outside Marseille serves as a hub to the region for budget airlines such as EasyJet and Ryanair. Aéroport Nantes Atlantique serves as a French base for the Spanish budget airline, Volotea.

SAINT MALO & MONT ST-MICHEL TRAVEL GUIDE

🌐 Currency

France's currency is the Euro. It is issued in notes in denominations of €500, €200, €100, €50, €20, €10 and €5. Coins are issued in €2, €1, 50c, 20c, 10c, 5c, 2c and 1c.

🌐 Banking & ATMs

If your ATM card is compatible with the MasterCard/Cirrus or Visa/Plus networks and configured for a 4-digit PIN, you will have no problem drawing money in France. Most French ATMs have an English language option. Remember to inform your bank of your travel plans before you leave. Keep an eye open around French ATMs to avoid pickpockets or scammers.

🌐 Credit Cards

Credit cards are frequently used throughout France, not just in shops, but also to pay for metro tickets, parking tickets, and motorway tolls and even to make phone calls at phone booths. MasterCard and Visa are accepted by most vendors. American Express and Diners Club are also accepted by the more tourist oriented businesses. Credit cards issued in Europe are smart cards that that are fitted with a microchip and require a PIN for each transaction. This means that a few ticket machines, self-service vendors and other businesses may not be configured to accept the older magnetic strip credit cards.

🌐 Tourist Taxes

All visitors to France pay a compulsory city tax or tourist tax ("taxe de séjour"), which is payable at your accommodation. Children are exempt from tourist tax. The rate depends on the standard of accommodation, starting with €0.75 per night for cheaper establishments going up to €4, for the priciest options. Rates are, of course, subject to change.

🌐 Reclaiming VAT

If you are not from the European Union, you can claim back VAT (or Value Added Tax) paid on your purchases in France. The VAT rate in France is 20 percent on most goods, but restaurant goods, food, transport and medicine are charged at lower rates. VAT can be claimed back on purchases of over €175 from the same shop, provided that your stay in France does not exceed six months. Look for shops that display a "Tax Free" sign. The shop assistant must fill out a form for reclaiming VAT. When you submit it at the airport, you can expect your refund to be debited within 30 to 90 days to your credit card or bank account. It can also be sent by cheque.

🌐 Tipping Policy

In French restaurants, a 15 percent service charge is added directly to your bill and itemized with the words *service compris* or "tip included". This is a legal requirement for taxation purposes. If the service was unusually good, a little extra will be appreciated. In an expensive restaurant where there is a coat check, you may add €1 per coat. In a few other situations, a tip will be appreciated. You can give an usherette in a theatre 50 cents to €1, give a porter €1 per bag for helping with your luggage or show your appreciation for a taxi driver with 5-10 percent over the fare. It is also customary to tip a hair dresser or a tour guide 10 percent.

🌐 Mobile Phones

Most EU countries, including France uses the GSM mobile service. This means that most UK phones and some US and Canadian phones and mobile devices will work in France. While you could check with your service provider about coverage before you leave, using your own service in roaming mode will involve additional costs. The alternative is to purchase a French SIM card to use during your stay in France. France has four mobile networks. They are Orange, SFR, Bouygues Telecom and Free. In France, foreigners are barred from applying for regular phone contract and the data rates are somewhat pricier on pre-paid phone services than in most European countries. You will need to show some form of identification, such as a passport when you make your purchase and it can take up to 48 hours to activate a French SIM card. If there is an Orange Boutique nearby, you can buy a SIM for €3.90. Otherwise, the Orange Holiday package is available for €39.99. Orange also sells a 4G device which enables your own portable Wi-Fi hotspot for €54.90. SFR offers a SIM card, simply known as le card for €9.99. Data rates begin at €5 for 20Mb.

Dialling Code

The international dialling code for France is +33.

Emergency Numbers

All emergencies: (by mobile) 112
Police: 17
Medical Assistance: 15
Fire and Accidents: 18
SOS All Emergencies (hearing assisted: 114)
Visa: 0800 90 11 79
MasterCard: 0800 90 13 87
American Express: 0800 83 28 20

Public Holidays

1 January: New Year's Day (Nouvel an / Jour de l'an / Premier de l'an)

SAINT MALO & MONT ST-MICHEL TRAVEL GUIDE

March - April: Easter Monday (Lundi de Pâques)

1 May: Labor Day (Fête du Travail / Fête des Travailleurs)

8 May: Victory in Europe Day (Fête de la Victoire)

May: Ascension Day (Ascension)

May: Whit Monday (Lundi de Pentecôte)

14 July: Bastille Day (Fête nationale)

15 August: Assumption of Mary (L'Assomption de Marie)

1 November: All Saints Day (La Toussaint)

11 November: Armistace Day (Armistice de 1918)

25 December: Christmas Day (Noël)

Good Friday and St Stephens Day (26 December) are observed only in Alsace and Moselle.

🌐 Time Zone

France falls in the Central European Time Zone. This can be calculated as Greenwich Mean Time/Co-ordinated Universal Time (GMT/UTC) +2; Eastern Standard Time (North America) -6; Pacific Standard Time (North America) -9.

🌐 Daylight Savings Time

Clocks are set forward one hour on the last Sunday of March and set back one hour on the last Sunday of October for Daylight Savings Time.

SAINT MALO & MONT ST-MICHEL TRAVEL GUIDE

🌐 School Holidays

The academic year in France is from the beginning of September to the end of June. The long summer holiday is from the beginning of July to the end of August. There are three shorter vacation periods. All schools break up for a two week break around Christmas and New Year. There are also two week breaks in February and April, but this varies per region, as French schools are divided into three zones, which take their winter and spring vacations at different times.

🌐 Driving Laws

The French drive on the ride hand side of the road. If you have a non-European driving licence, you will be able to use it in France, provided that the licence is valid and was issued in your country of residence before the date of your visa application. There are a few other provisions. The minimum driving age in France is 18. Your licence will need to be in French or alternately, you must carry a French translation of your driving permit with you.

In France, the speed limit depends on weather conditions. In dry weather, the speed limit is 130km per hour for highways, 110km per hour for 4-lane expressways and 90km per hour for 2 or 3-lane rural roads. In rainy weather, this is reduced to 110km, 100km and 80km per hour respectively. In foggy weather with poor visibility, the speed limit is 50km per hour on all roads. On urban roads, the speed limit is also 50km per hour.

By law, French drivers are obliged to carry a breathalyser in their vehicle, but these are available from most supermarkets, chemists and garages for €1. The legal limit is 0.05, but for new drivers who have had their licence for less than three years, it is 0.02. French motorways are called autorouts. It is illegal in France to use a mobile phone while driving, even if you have a headset.

Drinking Laws

The legal drinking age in France is 18. The drinking policy regarding public spaces will seem confusing to outsiders. Each municipal area imposes its own laws. In Paris, alcohol consumption is only permitted in licensed establishments. It is strictly forbidden in parks and public gardens.

Smoking Laws

From 2007, smoking has been banned in indoor spaces such as schools, government buildings, airports, offices and factories in France. The ban was extended in 2008 to hospitality venues such as restaurants, bars, cafes and casinos. French trains have been smoke free since December 2004.

SAINT MALO & MONT ST-MICHEL TRAVEL GUIDE

🌐 Electricity

Electricity: 220-240 volts

Frequency: 50 Hz

Electricity sockets in France are unlike those of any other country. They are hermaphroditic, meaning that they come equipped with both prongs and indents. When visiting from the UK, Ireland, the USA or even another European country, you will need a special type of adaptor to accommodate this. If travelling from the USA, you will also need a converter or step-down transformer to convert the current to to 110 volts, to avoid damage to your appliances. The latest models of many laptops, camcorders, mobile phones and digital cameras are dual-voltage with a built in converter.

🌐 Food & Drink

France is a paradise for dedicated food lovers and the country has a vast variety of well-known signature dishes. These include foie gras, bouillabaisse, escargots de Bourgogne, Coq au vin, Bœuf Bourguignon, quiche Lorraine and ratatouille. A great budget option is crêpes or pancakes. Favorite sweets and pastries include éclairs, macarons, mille-feuilles, crème brûlée and croissants.

The country is home to several world-famous wine-growing regions, including Alsace, Bordeaux, Bourgogne, Champagne,

SAINT MALO & MONT ST-MICHEL TRAVEL GUIDE

Corse, Côtes du Rhône, Languedoc-Roussillon, Loire, Provence and Sud-Ouest and correctly matching food to complimentary wine choices is practically a science. Therein lies the key to enjoying wine as the French do. It accompanies the meal. Drinking wine when it is not lunch or dinner time is sure to mark you as a foreigner. Pastis and dry vermouth are popular aperitifs and favorite after-dinner digestifs include cognac, Armagnac, calvados and eaux de vie. The most popular French beer is Kronenbourg, which originates from a brewery that dates back to 1664.

Websites

http://www.rendezvousenfrance.com/

http://www.france.com/

http://www.francethisway.com/

http://www.france-voyage.com/en/

http://www.francewanderer.com/

http://wikitravel.org/en/France

http://www.bonjourlafrance.com/index.aspx

Printed in Great Britain
by Amazon